THE LAST TWO SECONDS

BOOKS BY MARY JO BANG

Poetry

The Last Two Seconds
The Bride of E
Elegy
The Eye Like a Strange Balloon
The Downstream Extremity of the Isle of Swans
Louise in Love
Apology for Want

Translation

Inferno by Dante Alighieri

THE LAST TWO SECONDS

POEMS

Mary Jo Bang

Graywolf Press

This publication is made possible, in part, by the voters of Minnesota through a Minnesota State Arts Board Operating Support grant, thanks to a legislative appropriation from the arts and cultural heritage fund, and through grants from the National Endowment for the Arts and the Wells Fargo Foundation Minnesota. Significant support has also been provided by Target, the McKnight Foundation, Amazon.com, and other generous contributions from foundations, corporations, and individuals. To these organizations and individuals we offer our heartfelt thanks.

Published by Graywolf Press
250 Third Avenue North, Suite 600
Minneapolis, Minnesota 55401

www.graywolfpress.org

Published in the United States of America

ISBN 978-1-55597-704-7

2 4 6 8 9 7 5 3 1
First Graywolf Printing, 2015

Library of Congress Control Number: 2014950982

Cover design: Jeenee Lee Design

Cover art: Kikuzo Ito, *Speeding Monorail: On the Precipice,* 1936

CONTENTS

THE LAST TWO SECONDS

THE EARTHQUAKE SHE SLEPT THROUGH

She slept through the earthquake in Spain.
The day after was full of dead things. Well, not full but a few.
Coming in the front door, she felt the crunch of a carapace

under her foot. In the bathroom, a large cockroach rested
on its back at the edge of the marble surround; the dead
antennae announced the future by pointing to the silver mouth

that would later gulp the water she washed her face with.
Who wouldn't have wished for the quick return
of last night's sleep? The idea, she knew, was to remain awake,

and while walking through the day's gray fog, trick the vaporous
into acting like something concrete: a wisp of cigarette smoke,
for instance, could become a one-inch Lego building

seen in the window of a bus blocking the street.
People sometimes think of themselves as a picture that matches
an invented longing: a toy forest, a defaced cricket, the more

or less precious lotus. The night before the quake, she took a train
to see a comic opera with an unlikely plot. She noticed a man
in a tan coat and necktie who looked a lot like Kafka.

The day after, she called a friend to complain about the bugs.
From a distant city—his voice low and slightly plaintive—he said,
"Are you not well? Is there anything you want?"

COSTUMES EXCHANGING GLANCES

        The rhinestone lights blink off and on.
Pretend stars.
I'm sick of explanations. A life is like Russell said
of electricity, not a thing but the way things behave.
A science of motion toward some flat surface,
some heat, some cold. Some light
can leave some after-image but it doesn't last.
Isn't that what they say? That and that
historical events exchange glances with nothingness.

YOU KNOW

You know, don't you, what we're doing here?
The evening laid out like a beach ball gone airless.

We're watching the spectators in the bleachers.
The one in the blue shirt says, "I knew,

even as a child, that my mind was adding color
to the moment."

The one in red says, "In the dream, there was a child
batting a ball back and forth. He was chanting

that awful rhyme about time that eventually ends
with the body making a metronome motion."

By way of demonstration, he moves mechanically
side to side while making a clicking noise.

His friends look away. They all know
how a metronome goes. You and I continue to watch

because we have nothing better to do.
We wait for the inevitable next: we know the crowd

will rise to its feet when prompted and count—
one-one-hundred, two-one-hundred,

three-one-hundred—as if history were a sound
that could pry apart an ever-widening abyss

with a sea on the bottom. And it will go on like this.
The crowd will quiet when the sea reaches us.

MASQUERADE: AFTER BECKMANN

We're sitting here quietly.
You're feeling your arm, I'm feeling my face.
We're supposed to stay quiet
and live the waiting life.

We were told to be a portraitist's object
and imitate a sad fate.
We are a skull times two.
We're supposed to stay quiet.

Herr Moment is looking
at a watch that says now.
Its red face reminds me of the eye of an ogre.
Its shiny rim reminds me

of Herr Moment's handcuffs.
I don't want to speak
about what can't be fathomed—
mourning and missing, rings cut from corpses,

Herr Moment's refusal to show his real face.

AT THE MOMENT OF BEGINNING

1.

A cage can be a body: heart in the night
quieted slightly; mind, a stopped top.
Clock spring set. Hand in motion.
The fact of the hollowed nothing head.

How did we come to this? Inch by inch.
I was born, borrowed from the beast;
I was now property in a country
where chain reigns—the empire city of I.

2.

So, the empire: the breath, the legend
Of the well-guarded hell.
One comes to tell you
what you should have done differently.

I think, I say, and I am not you.
In the margin of fear I heard a woman
convincing me to listen.
"Listen," she said, "to the doctor."

3.

The city before this was nothing
but swirled sand in a storm.
Nothing turns back. I saw a fluttering
I recognized in the distance.

Out of nowhere, there was red:
the furnace and the beating heart.
Every giddy excess behind the beginning
was also leading to the emphatic end.

WALL STREET

The trapeze artist above
                     is invested in space.
She attends to the arc the bar makes
                     the way you'd watch a movie
where a star who looks like you swings on a swing.

It's true you know how to wait
                     although I don't know that
that counts as knowledge.

I heard a banker say to Monsignor this morning,
                     I'm certain God wishes me well.

        A rat's face at the window next to me
        is stone and the wind isn't blowing.
        A rat's face sometimes reminds me
        of what one sees in a morning mirror:
        nose, eyes, a head, some hair.
        Five racehorses, neck to neck,
        each with four feet off the ground:
        yet another classic example
        of time seeming to be standing still.
        Everyone with money knows that
        flying from Pisa to France is a pain
        since you have to change planes in Brussels.
        As I said to Monsignor this morning,
        I'm certain God wishes me well.

THE STORM WE CALL PROGRESS

Strum and concept, drum and bitterness, the dog
of history keeps being blown into the present—
her back to the future, her last supper simply becoming
the bowels' dissolving memory in a heap before her.
A child pats her back and drones *there there*
while under her lifted skirt is a perfect today
where a cult of ghost-lovers predicts a rapture
but instead remains to inherit varicose veins,
rubber knickers, douches with bulbs, douches with bags,
girdles in a choice of pink, red or white,
and in rubber, silk or twilled linen, enemas, clysters, oils,
balms, and other Benjamin etceteras burrowing
like scabies into the brain's ear as it listens to the click
of the next second coming to an end.

                            Throughout,
the senseless waste of reaching up to pull down
a machine-made device from the rafters, a beatific
mythical magical deity. *Sturm und Drang*, storm
and stress, turbulence and urge, turmoil and ferment.
A revolution goes right, then wrong. The right falls
in love with an icon. They force the landscape into a box.
They lock the box with the key inside. The aristocracy
is an improbable agent of change. Whispering
is no longer saying out loud, the all-seeing god a brother
grown bigger by another name.
Adv. sadly
He stared sadly at the ruins of his house. *traurig*
Er starrte traurig auf die Ruinen seines Hauses. sadly

PROVISIONAL DOUBT AS AN ARCHITECTURAL SPACE

People make the mistake of thinking of impossibility
as if it were a corner visible dimly through a blanket

called "a failed way of thinking." I see the impossible
as an example of the simulacra

that demands that you decide whether it is a new thing,
or simply the old thing emptied of itself.

Remembering the impossible is like remembering
a struggle that shows no signs of struggle but is a record

of a permanent closed door that always looks
as if it just happened. The scene is the early 1960s:

a room, a fog-gray wall, an absence of ambition
as a response to self-doubt. Along the way, the ceremony

of switching on a light, setting a table, the ordinary useless
shapes of the nonchalant. Meanwhile,

the room keeps disappearing like some relentless nothing.

THE TOO-BRIGHT LIGHT WILL WASH YOU OUT

Some photo solution to dissipation, wasting,
some erase of face, some get out of here
and keep going. The sun bleaching you dark
and gone.

But before that you're asleep and dream-sorting
through what will be left behind. A closetful
of dried grass, and a jacket. Two boxes of what.
You've come so far. You've come a long way.

You've gone and you don't stop going.
A year filled with this day, this, this, this day, this,
this becoming a form of sidling up to cessation.
This day, this. Winter will bring emptiness,

emptiness, emptiness; winter will bring emptiness.
All spring, emptiness. All summer. All fall.

AN INDIVIDUAL EQUINOX SUITABLE FOR FRAMING

She is sitting in front of a plate. On it, fresh lettuce and better—a handful of murmur and stir spinning in circles. She offers herself a word of advice: Don't. Says, you'll only pitch forward and start receding into a figure paused to reflect on what's outside the window. Cars backed up for miles. Firefly taxi-light flicker.

The sea, if it ever was, is gone. A rhythmic geometry troubles the horizon. She spends too much time looking at a tree. She sees it but doesn't know it. Which is something like the idea of freedom: it's impossible to achieve and yet the individual sometimes *feels* free. Inside the mind a vector points to someone subtly rustling the wormhole, which in turn makes her wonder: who is that? Who was that me?

> Light under the sky, the window all but closed,
> disarray inside, pale gray near white out,
> a stone stock-still moment, and then motion,
> a woman in that faint place, a surrender to
>
> what can't be escaped. A kind of ever-rest.
> Anatomy enough to accommodate
> departure in segments, thousands of questions.
> The architecture isn't only belated
>
> it's entirely gone and in its place a green
> that looks nothing like a life was lived there.
> Examples, names, dates, seen
> flowers, irises edging a back wall. Where?
>
> Yes, everything said not once but several times.
> The flowers coming back in different colors
> like communications sound various, dimes
> and metal buttons spilled on the counter,
>
> fast film blurred to capture low light. Strange
> everywhere. Day collapsing into equal night.

EQUIDISTANT FROM THE CENTER OF NEVER

The door closed on the self she had been and
the outside went soft. A cat brushed by a leg.

A car went over a cliff. The clock minutia stopped
and was hours ahead when she opened her eyes.

The sky opened and let out an image: the optical
illusion of a mountain melting, each former rock

now a bird in the mouth of a cat, or something
like that. Countless snare wires fired in succession,

a tornado continually mimed a bluster on one side
or the other of audible. Everything lasted a second.

RUDE MECHANICALS

       Against a white wall
someone's hair was a treetop; the body,
a trunk. It was a time
when everyone said,

"Behind every great veil is only a human."
If there was an overall ethos, it was
self-forgetful guilt and sorrow was real
enough. "I don't know how

the curtain caught fire," she'd said.
And I don't know how reluctance to act
became a machine sucking air
from every sulcus and Grand Canyon

canyon. "Do you like air?"
What could one say to that—
I'll have to think about it?
The waiter came by with the pepper mill.

The barman with his cocktail shaker.
The unsaid was becoming a picture
of sand, land, and nothing.
It was inevitable, she said, that she would

someday stand behind bars
at a window. She could imagine it:
high above an ice-covered expanse
otherwise covered with tin men

and tin women and rude mechanicals.
The noise, she was sure, would be awful.

THE CIRCUS WATCHER

I wear red to match the air
that comes over the fence
and fills the jar in which I keep the day.
I say every dog looks like no other
but that isn't true. Not entirely.
Difference is slippery. I say,

Just look at my head, how it tilts to look up
at these over-large leaves. They're large
and blue, the better to be seen
by my pincushion eye, so bright in the light.
I am sad. I am happy. I keep busy.
I count the eight legs of the tick

on the table. Arachnid and such.
The book I leave open, the wind blows it shut.
In late April I make a schedule: June
to July, July to August. I begin to realize
the circus will be places, minds, people,
pleasure. The drumming all of these.

I practice, when I'm not sure of myself,
this repetition: know, know, know, knew.
I think that chaos fascinates me. I say,
I am part of that,
one of the characters in a cage.

SILENCE ALWAYS HAPPENS SUDDENLY

She had been talking about the story
where the cat had been belled.

Now the cat sat alone, learning.
Why learn behaving, slinking, fetching?
Why? No reply. The telephone rang.

It's the biology mistress, the cat said.

The fine-print zeitgeist was act,
and consequence—
a mirror-image inference, the perfect mate.

The clear message was: the world's full
of fear, finessed slightly more.

Death, said the cat, as it lifted a souvenir
trinket mermaid castle from the fish tank,

is day plummeting
behind a cruise missile set for a mid-sized city.

PRACTICE FOR BEING EMPTY

I'm only a human. Always is only in me
as long as I last. What do I want? Don't ask.

We forget who we are. Conformists all alone
looking for a fake mirror and finding it
in some poker-faced nobody

sitting across the aisle. To be like some other
and feel that while I am walking around
on the only surface that exists in here—

some stage set designed for collapsing.
While I don't the world falls away.
This circus I'm part of was built just for this.

AN AUTOPSY OF AN ERA

That's how it was then, a knife
through cartilage, a body broken. Animal
and animal as mineral ash. A window smashed.
The collective howl as a general alarm
followed by quiet.

                    Boot-black night,
halogen hum. Tape snaking through
a stealth machine. Later, shattered glass
and a checkpoint charm—the clasp
of a tourist-trap bracelet. An arm. A trinket.

Snap goes the clamshell. The film
in the braincase preserving the sense
of the drench, the angle of the leash,
the connecting collar. A tracking long-shot.
The descent of small-town darkness.

A CALCULATION BASED ON FIGURES IN A SCENE

There are still many marvels, you know.
The festivals on Fridays. The divider
in the center of the wasteland.
On this side—flesh; on that—an iron claw

and a new-made screw
fallen from the factory window
at noon. The doll doctor pushes the arm
back into the socket. "There," he says.

Day is done. He wishes he could smoke
but he gave that up long ago.
The rubber sole of the nurse's right shoe
makes a squeak when she reaches the room.

Silence surrounds the empty bed.
The body is elsewhere.
"When they want more," she says, "I give it."
"When they want less," she says,

"I take it away. I always let them choose."
The doctor drums his fingers
on the doll's flat abdomen. A sea of blood
moves back and forth to a song of no mercy.

THE NUMBERS

I'm making a strudel of bluebirds.
A pied piper is playing a strange song
to the sound of a shredder that's going non-stop,
each ordinal number is isolated, each receipt
gets eaten. Each is made safe.
The dish is hot from the oven.
The mesmerizing sound lulls like a candle
on a table makes a mirror of the eye.
A knife draws a line down the center.
This is mine. This is yours.
There is no way out.
Every language gets speckled with references
to what it is to be after: shredded,
sleeping—eyes closed, home-schooled
to ignore what you don't want to see.
Now, down the disposal the feathers,
the unfed, the crust crumbs,
the monogrammed small plates stamped I
for Idiocy. Mine and yours.
After the fall of the Wall I felt anything
was possible. History would no longer exist.

The mic goes out.
The sound softens.
The books burn down to embers, then ash.
The fever hospital closes for lack
of a solution to the seven deadly sins: betrayal
for one, intolerance for two,
greed for three, cruelty for four, large cars
for five, war for six, suicide for seven
when it kills more than one.

LIONS AND TIGERS: THE ESCAPED ANIMAL WAS BENT TO THE TRAINER'S WILL

We put you in the circus. Was that a good idea? And now
there are so few of you. Why why why why why?
Why why why why why why?

CAN THE INDIVIDUAL EXPERIENCE TRAGIC CONSEQUENCES?

A human head should infold
        to behold all extremes: monstrous

serpents, lambs joined
            with dolphins, the sea,

flowing hair, a nose, eyes.
The forest dies,

and
       we are mice in the midst of things.

THE BLANK OF REASON PRODUCES BLANK: AFTER GOYA

Now reversal inches back into the past:
bomb building and bloodbath.
A billion anthills in a grid.
Drone and bass blasting every chorda tympani.
Flesh melting. The sky moving a mushroom.
The stupid apprentice at a loss to sweep water
and staunch his watch. My head's in my hands.
Some sobbing from somewhere. Is it you?
You vote but the vote goes nowhere.
Dante to Virgil, "I can't bear to listen any longer."
Night of crystal, night of knives, day of wall
plus wire, morning falling into a reeking cloud
of time burning back to liquid, to rock declining
like gravity in a glass shattering.
Someone comes in in a white coat.
In my white coat.
I call myself doctor but really, I'm consequence.
The winter of consequence. I can't learn.

THE PERPETUAL NIGHT SHE WENT INTO

She went into the perpetual theatrical night
and woke somewhere past the point of fading
but before sunlight was due to be reinstated. Afterward,

a small wish that she could lie down and close her eyes
at the side of yesterday's quarry-cut rock. In her mind,
she was the weather—i.e., an inconsistent frenzy,

intermittently electric, insistently wedded
to Monday's tower of wooden blocks. The sharp pinch
of some maybes. She thought, I've felt this. I think

it's the furniture in the gloom for some of us.
Her deportment got ordered from time to time.
A jury decided that a wave should sweep over her again.

She marveled at a wall in the optician's office: eye chart,
frames missing lenses arranged in rows. Very classic, yet
disquieting. She looked at it over and over until whatever

was was letter perfect with no corrections. This,
while outside a talking hammered hailstorm bounced up
and domed a column of men coming down the sidewalk.

EXCEPT FOR BEING, IT WAS RELATIVELY PAINLESS

It was relatively painless except for being all she could see: a world made of dinner, very pleasant; a lunch at something called a table in the dining room; an endless night; a half-day; another lunch, this on Tuesday. Yesterday. Today. Pieces propped up with supports. The therapist tapped his cigar. He no longer accepted her general opposition to myth, marriage, Olympic Games, and the course of decades. He said it was as if she were engaged in an eternal war, either watching a movie or acting in one, depending on the situation and time of day. She sat in silence, the sky above a half-baked blue, a blank-face dying of awkwardness. The simple explanation boiled down to the too-easy explanation. He was smart and charming then; and later, much less so. Behind his head, pictures were crammed together with the top layer hung so high she had to crane her neck to see the details. He said to please pretend she was listening.

TIME TRAP: THE PERPETUAL MOMENT

Sandwiched between the sidewalk and an upper floor,
she was drinking in an afternoon that was making her
uneasy. The situation was further complicated
by the proximity to the dilemma
of whether to chance the unstable elevator.
How else to get back to where she'd begun?
It occurred to her that every dilemma
goes into the river of consciousness with lipstick on
a tissue, a rat in the basement, a man on the street.
Meanwhile, someone was talking to her
while first names kept flashing by in a cracked mirror
whenever she blinked. Across the room, a man
who looked like a younger form of Freud was saying,
"—consciousness-wise, the doctor is no worse
and no better than a novel
that wants you to know every chapter
once was titled 'The Moment Is the State Suspended.'"

HAD THERE BEEN

There had been a particularly disturbing dream
the night before. Awake, the associations led to something
she'd read about the Audubon Society in the *Times*, which led
to years ago, when she came down from the city and saw A—
in Philadelphia, A— saying she hadn't liked her daughter
until later. The shock of that. The shock also of what someone
can become. She said she gardened now. She was surprised
she still remembered that. Blind slats let in an inch or so of sun
times the length of the window. Outside the sigh of a braking bus,
the length of the street times once upon a time. The story began,
"This is the corner where the murder took place." Of course, corner
could be parking garage, or an off-track betting parlor. Murders
happen everywhere, even inside the brain, a moment of anger
and just like that the other is over.

A MAN MENTIONED IN AN ESSAY

She began with the premise that the world was
an unbroken overlay of dust motes
and added to that only what she could see:
a bird eats corn and becomes.
It's true if you see a platypus in a glass case,
you remember. A layer of thinking makes ideas
go forward until the latch at the end of the day
where sleep gets attached to fading,
the loop set on auto-alert for a future waking.
She knew she was one of countless others,
any of which one might meet and soon forget.
There was no reason it should be otherwise.
The essay mentioned a man, an interview,
a train, fingerprints, photo, shoes, and
a red sweater. The future was quite irresistible,
it washed over you. Because, she said, is a way
of pointing to the apparent reason that,
in a trial in which the complaint concerns
the terms of human behavior.
She didn't notice the year's ending. Then
shortly after midnight, she heard noises outside
and realized it was the muffled repetitive boom
of distant fireworks. Good-bye to that, she said.

LET'S SAY YES

1. SCENE AFTER SCENE

I love pictures. Scene after scene
shooting to a brain. Messages on waves.
But suddenly, in the middle of day, an arrow
like a knife through a perpetual instant.
The only gift was instinct:
a cat's plodding, a glove of nothing.

White dawn. This idiocy. Throw of the dice
but not this red upright jar,
this violent explosion,
a dove-grey shop like a cloud, falling upon faces.
Whose? Nobody. A standstill,
the throb of a pulse,

a curious pattern. Some horror-world
blocking the pavement but for the cars
on both sides. The symbol
of a grass-grown path hurrying along,
at the top, copies of wheels.
A crowd of thighs without occupation.

High up the sound of white smoke for a moment.
Awestricken, perfectly still,
a grasshopper's rasped spine transfixed,
shut eyes, alive but robbed of suspense.
The outlines gone, the night is full of daylight.
Midnight boundaries lost.

Animals stretched over the zoo.
The cricket voice of the suffering. Stone men,
women, spread out on the steps of society.
The traffic. The swish
of exquisite moments, while by her, trying
to calm, a weapon sliced the surface,

ripped the man and woman confessing to some
sudden revelation, an illumination.
Blood in veins had to be amazing.
The sponge of feeling. Pink evening.
A granite wall. Falling.

2. THIS BELL LIKE A BEE STRIKING

Exactly, thought. Here she is having a mind,
a moon ghastly light on a person. To suffer
emotion, throat stiff, child grown larger.
A whole. Summoned so one can have a look.
Summoned to husband what's happened.

The light challenged the powers
of feeling: frightening, exhilarating, surprise,
shame. It was over. Plaster and litter alone.
Five acts that had been.
Over and over. A strange power speaking.

Some concern for the half-past. Ring after ring
like something coming. It is thought,
this bell like a bee striking.
The future lies in a patter like a wood drummed.
A sensual traffic: what, where, and why.

Three emotions. Shutters and avenues.
The red burning. A lizard's color in her eyes.
Evening wearing the fringes in the windows.
The light wavering in the darkness streets.
Atoms turned. Thinking like the pulse—

punctually, noiselessly silk.
Ridiculous. Her mother grown big.
She, like most mothers, a swept shuffle
of traffic and dress and nothing
except the flutter of absolution.

Such are things merged. The cupboard outline
becomes soft. A table. Cigarette smoke.
A baby bright pink. Daring with being.
That dog. Lots of coldness. Yet, some power
to preside with her head, with her shoulders,

through dinner. A sort of maternal politics.
Her dress disappearing. Sweeping off for bed
with headaches. Still, the sun. The squirrels.
Pebbles to the pebble collection. She blinks
at the crack of a twig behind the bedroom walls.

3. THE NERVE FIBERS

The nerve fibers, a veil on red music clanging,
cannoned from columns. An anthem bubbling.

Scientifically stretching over the cheeks
at the edge of one moment. The grey suit passed,

the overcoat, impressions everywhere.
Watching a negligible dog fetch as if it were human—

his hind legs so honest, so independent—
she stood in a doorway, not beautiful, never

specially clever, remote from herself. Over and over—
twist, turn, wake up, set going. Doomed to sinking—

decorate the dungeon, be decent.
The edge of her mind turning meaning for hours

at a time. Hours and days. A sound like a sickle.
Her head a bunch of heather. Then over.

The matted and tangled message, a red square.
The thinking nerves. The door of the room.

Dante : the Inferno. The English : London.
A piston thumping mechanically behind the screen.

Mixed clouds and seagulls, grey circles interlocked.
Grey to grey nothing nervous system.

4. TO WRITE A HISTORY

A sister adoring shrouds,
Some institutions, uneasiness. Likeness
in a type of story. A photograph, *Table*—
by the Committee of the Physically Existent.

The answer is to go beneath life:
here was the door opened,
the door ajar. And outside was history:
engraving of a sofa, a factory, violin sound.

The dwindling impulse. The gigantic clock.
The clock was her mind.

5. OPENED AND SHUT

She had prepared a looking-glass: hair, dress, thought,
sofa in the glow of dogs barking.

Beautifully close up. And once, flames
eating the edge of the sofa.

Her eyelashes blurred. Chin, nose, forehead, some lips.
The cheek. The glass looking first at one thing,
then another: nose, eyes, evening.

She sat looking at the map of her hands.
The window, the clock, her pulse.

The body was busy thinking, conjuring
the museum of a moment: emotion, scenes, people,
bags of treasures. Heaps of theories.

Theories to explain feeling the here and the back of the hand.
A theory allowed one thing after another.
First, dinner, then morning.

Her hand was the world.
To get to it she had to look at herself.

To get at the truth one would have to disregard
anything false. Yet the truth was intangible.

One eye on the horizon: a long indeterminable,
mere straightness, a few plants,
that indescribable purple.

Doors being opened. Visual impressions—
as if the eye were the brain, the body entering the house.

6. THERE SHE WAS

The house stood. The cars were standing.
She was walking over to the dog
which had to be remembered.
"Shake hands," she said. He straightened,
bent, straightened.
His manner was irreproachable,
that being with a tail.

It was extraordinary, life was.
Furs being petted, people standing upright,
panic, fear, tight skirts, ankles, thought.
The creature standing, her giving little pats.
She was enjoying standing there.
She had forgotten this feeling.
Ordinary things—curtains, biscuits, bones,

a creature raising one foreleg, the movies.
She stood looking as if she would solidify—
Darwin draped in black
remembering the flora or fauna.
Of course, she would really only
be remembering a garden, trees, wallpaper,
a sea-lion barking, a doctor of misery

on the verge of difficulty. A boy gone. Death.
Death without life. Terror. Fear. Disaster.
Punishment. Profound darkness. Evening.
She walked to the window: sky,
clouds coming into the room.
How odd, she thought, to be.

EXPLAIN THE BRAIN

Individuate the particular
and you get a slice of totality: the car, for instance,
becomes a composite of separate parts: gears,

tank, hubcaps, paint coat, mudflaps, a clock,
a divided dash. New example: a neuron.
You could say the brain works

from knowledge and ambiguity.
Radical fundamentalism is not supportable
by appeal to the best.

Why then is fundamentalism common:
reductive explanations induce the pleasure
of misunderstanding?

A weak ego lacks distinct boundaries?
There are other ways of thinking?
Take Aristotle's example of a rooster and the sun

and substitute a shadow and a flagpole.
The brain has elements in common with cameras
but isn't one. A collection of biochemical cascades

over components that span the membrane
results in behavior at the fundamental level.
Sometimes one is wrong.

THE EARTHQUAKE IN THIS CASE WAS

a seismic storm that knocked down
buildings—the buildings teetering before falling
the way ideologies might sway back and forth

if they were preserved in a glass tower
that was about to be toppled. In any storm,
one hopes he or she is bound in advance

by the story line to escape at the end. In speech,
the mouth becomes a wheelbarrow
that can assert its contents.

The tool-and-die exactitude of pre-packaged thought
is estranging because it suggests
the discrete elements can't be teased apart.

Blind faith relies on an obedience that verges
on boredom. Any disquiet, however slight, might
define a moment like a character's obsessive cough

might define a character by exploding
when it shouldn't. It keeps exploding
and when it does it acts in the story

like a glass box cracked by a hammer that breaks
and becomes a broken box. In both situations,
action releases the stale air encased there.

And now the question: what do we do with the longing
for what can destroy us? You're free to think:
logic can change even the most obstinate person; or,

even logic cannot change the most obstinate person.

TWO PLACES AND ONE TIME

A palimpsest is something with something
behind it. Behind her was a plan and a face
in a window at night that essentially said, You see

yourself where you're not.
She began as a set of sketches
for the construction of a traumatized body

fresh from birth with the mouth removed.
The room went light and dark. The sun narrowed.
She put on her shoes.

Think about it, she thought, a diagram
has no predictive value.
A blueprint can't keep a house from falling.

The magic of glass shows where one is
even when one is not.
Which is to say, I live inside a scene

inside my head: a lake that remains water
except in winter when the rough cover
of white waves to someone driving by in a car.

A cigarette thrown from the window burns down
to the filter. It maintains its shape but becomes ash.
Gray replaces white.

Whenever she left the room
the touch of her fingers on the broken lock
extended the realm of being in there.

TWO FRAMES

In one sense, you could say I was framed—in other words, led
into circumstances I wouldn't otherwise have found myself in.
But that wouldn't be the whole story.
You want me to "shed" light on it?

I can tell you now, that will never happen. I will say this,
the situation wasn't some pink angora cardigan
with mother-of-pearl buttons that slip into the slot
they were made for just because you find yourself "a little chilly"

after a day at the beach, a little burned on the back,
at least the top of your shoulders. You found yourself wishing
again (didn't you?) for some Polaroid moment
of the past when girls always sunned under umbrellas

and mascara stayed where you wanted it to. I can tell you that
will never happen again. We're post-postmodern—in the city,
anyway. We know where we are going and it isn't back and forth.
We want and light comes. We call what we want what we need.

A TECHNICAL DRAWING OF THE MOMENT

Before the monument becomes remote
and unapproachable, a made-up anecdote
of easy adoration, pressed into marble
or a more modern plastic, let's ask ourselves,
What is myth? And further, is it better
to dispel or debunk one, or instead
should we embrace the petty mechanistic
hope that invents it? Are we not ridiculous,
torn in two between the true
and what we'd so like to believe is true?
It's exactly there, right where we keep our wishes,
that our fake animals act as a code
for what we think of as enlightenment. There,
a tiger's faux hide pretends to be a pelt that says,
This was my life. And so it was,
since a symbol is nothing but an illustration
of obsession, concern, focus, and an atlas
of where one wishes to have been
or fears one someday will go.
Color can add detail to the expanse between
the short but bright beginning of an era
and a mottled much longer after.
History moves in under the glass-top
where from a safe distance we can watch it
become our keeper and contentious tormenter.
I admit to being frightened, or better,
ill at ease, with what I don't know but can see:
the instinct for power that some people have.

UNDER THE INFLUENCE OF IDEALS

The extra-fine ingredients sift down on you
or stir at your feet and cover your shoes
with dust. The back of your hands,
dusted. Some fine glass particles stick.
The long bath only removes the thin layer
that can be removed. Everything else
is taken in and kept. You stand up
when you can to the curled lip,
some dog-face raking back the curtain
to expose the starving. Who isn't on edge?
Always the look that says don't. And then,
the strategic repetition of the threat.
Death in the performance foreground,
some long-past allegory in back.
"Zero" plays on low while you look back
over your shoulder in a three-way mirror;
look up—there's the glass chandelier
that substitutes for a people on the edge
of their seats. The natural birthright
position. Every last scene lasts for no more
than a second; some ceramic panther
stands in for the extinct. Is it today yet?
On stage, in a moment of everyday realism,
an accordion folds and unfolds while
we pretend we forget we said we'd be kind.

THE LANDSCAPIST

Nothing has changed, especially
not stumbling. Watching
the play, I thought, this is sad.
This is sad. Affective moments crowd
into a consuming curiosity,
the medical journal says. And then
they asked the subjects: Do you sleep
well? Do you eat well? Do you work
without stimulants? They all said.
One described a house where
someone had summered. A square
tower. Easy driving distance.
Some unsigned damaged painting
on the back of which was another
retrieved from a landfill and later by
not much shoed into a dream
where blown-glass kitsch figures
were excavated from a pit.
Looking out the window above that
graveyard of unearthed history I saw.

ALL THROUGH THE NIGHT

The rotational earth, the resting for seconds:
hemisphere one meets hemisphere two,
thoughts twist apart at the center seam.
Everything inside is.
Cyndi Lauper and I both fall into pure emptiness.
That's one way to think: I think I am right now.
We have no past we won't reach back—
The clock ticks like the nails of a foiled dog
chasing a faster rabbit across a glass expanse.
A wheel of fortune spins on its side,
stops and starts. The stopped time
is no longer time, only an illusion that says,
I can have this, and this, and this.
Cyndi says nothing works like that.
There is no all-purpose plastic totem
that acts like a bouncer holding back the fact
that at least once a day you look up:
it's the self you kept in a suitcase holding the key,
coming to meet you, every cell a node
in a network of ongoing doubling. Cyndi says
the world expands but always keeps us in it.
For every you, there's a riot grrrl in prison
in Putin's Russia. You know the self dissolves
and when it does—no figure, all ground,
like a surface seen microscopically—
you fill the frame and explode,
a rubber-wound inside unraveling and becoming
a measurement of whatever exits. It's like sleep,
if sleep were a film that didn't include you, but no,
whatever is happening, you are always in it,
the indispensable point of view.
Proof of that is that a lift force brings you back
and you wake, back to your face, hands, mirror
image in the bed next to you, Ketamine moment
where kinesthesia is secondary to everything
is possible: you and you and you and now and
you and yes and you with the night-self singing

backup. Onstage, the fractured future of a world
which is the world with the scaffolding folded
and laid on top of this night. All through it.
Until it ends or else begins again. Meanwhile,
that indefatigable wavering between
what you want and what you get for wanting.

READING CONRAD'S *HEART OF DARKNESS*

1.

Think of yourself as a character. It's hot today,
in the house it's cooler. Cool air rises off the floor and meets
the heat that inches in through the window.

Listen to the cicadas, the monkeys.
Water evaporates. The boat is dragged forward
along a matched track—to what is that attached?

Today we will read a book and play in the right chamber.

2.

At 6:30 in the morning, there was the noise of the cicadas.
The bus was a lit interior filled with people on their way
to work as she walked in the dark. A man threw a pail of water

on the pavement. She went back to the hotel
and swam in a blue oval pool. The water was warm.
There was another woman there and the two of them spoke

about pleasure. The day before she left that city
she bought a carved ivory figurine at an antique shop
and smuggled it back to London in her suitcase.

Sometimes a person knows an act is wrong but does it anyway.
I myself sometimes don't know why I do a thing.
She wrapped it in a black sweater

and tucked it into a zippered pocket along the linear axis
of the side of the case. At the airport,
the customs official asked her to open her suitcase.

He patted her folded clothes, then closed the case.
The ivory figurine was "a lady doctor." In a former era
it was used to show the physician where the pain was

while protecting a woman's modesty. Months later,
her neighbor offered to take it with her when she went
to sell a landscape painting at an auction house.

The neighbor came back to say she'd been told it wasn't real;
she'd been told, she said, that it was a Victorian reproduction,
and worth approximately ninety pounds.

3.
Here's the boat: watch it move forward.
The motor sounds mechanical.
A light bleeds through the shade.

Look at the night to the right, scissored by lightning
Visible rain is whipping the window
with what feels like fury. Then straight rain with silence,

until the window is opened.
When the window is opened, there is the insistently real
sound of rain. The sound meets the eardrum and becomes

one with the body. It is as if nature is making a statement
that sometimes the outside and inside are one.
Darkness is only a relative

index of many other aspects of the way light behaves.
We know the convulsive reiterative mapping—*lub-dub,
lub-dub, lub-dub*—has multiple meanings.

4.
It hurts here, she says, and points to the torso.
The ivory woman lying on her side.
The doctor's unsettling warning sounds endlessly.

Thebesian: tragic stories with tragic endings.
Thebesian veins: tributaries
draining directly into the cardiac chambers.

The lightless interior filled with a thick liquid.
The rain was over. Contained.
The possibility of restitution occurs to the character.

The regardless night. Time's impossible stop. The stars
that predicted disaster. She was drawn back
to what she'd once seen on a stage: someone posing,

saying to the audience, "Look at me, I'm only made
of cardboard. What real good can I do?"

AS IN CORONA

Corona, as in the luminous,

gas plus liquids plus solids
that make up matter.
What's the matter? Right,
the coroner. The holder
of an office he inherited
from the crown. The bodies
of persons who died and were
cremated. Corporations are
bodies, so said the Court. What
about corpuscular blood? She
said, I once wore the couture
of the social counter-irritant
seeking to counter an unjust
war. Compurgation is the belief
in innocence that may or may
not be true. Truthiness, a word
recently made popular by
a comic who plays a pundit.
On television, at night, Coolidge
Dam often disappears and the
continent comes back to life.
It became the practice of the
Church in the west to withhold
the cup from the laity. More for
the cobra-headed pope. Who
said that? Complexion: a case of
pigment. Coney Island, a creek
filled in, a case of rabbits. Their
skins were so soft. Congress is
a body. See also sexual. Fire
raging through the multistoried
castle, destroying the crypt
where the state concealed

graphic messages about how to
manage cruelty. To animals. To
children. To some cribbage deck
of commoners, whose privilege
has been determined by the toss
of a coin out a window. Caught-
out means caught in deception.
Slaves were forced to cultivate
cash crops in Confederate States.
In the cabinet of silence, those
supported by liquidities and cash
and a cosmography of valuable
information—. They do or have
to do what? It's complicated.
There are conflicts, of course.
Cranes raise the question and we
look at it. And at this: the choir
stall where singers sing, "Raise
Your Hand If You Care to Think."
The ice crusted over the graves
now. The ash of an ice rink. The
men in earmuffs. The sorrowing
telescope. We are all alone, after
all. Madame Curie's death from
radium poisoning. The roaches
in her kitchen outlasting her.
The canary in the coalmine. An
eloquent Cassandra unlistened to.
Unbelieved by those who prefer
the palace of pure holy imagining.
Hypocrisy: to take the one crumb
from the hungry and in confusion
watch as they writhe in a cage.

A STRUCTURE OF REPEATING UNITS

A lamp is a great gift, I think.
The brass tack ouch of a hand
to a hot bulb takes you straight to the top
of the threshold of feeling. A small plastic
object held to the cheek is also quite nice.
I love poly socks, dishtowels with rick-rack,
a surfboard anointed with one aqua stripe.
Idle want seems to dog me along a long cord
that's plugged into the boot in the mouth
of the near recent past.
    The plastic,
we both know, is nothing but a patchwork
of particles, a mash-up of atoms, petroleum
before or after it's oil—but still, it means
so much more. Something finer than fine.
Like pearls bred from time and insouciance.
Or something like that. I turn out the light,
lock the door, lie down, brush my hair
from my forehead, and listen
for the cinematographer to say to the dark,
Just wait and the world will come back.
The terror I have, I keep hidden.

IN THIS BOX

Think of me as a plant stand turned animal.
Something to hold, or be held.
Think of a pandan matte black and white.
It's easy. Or at least not too terribly hard.
Think about the danger of night
as the lid of tomorrow tacked to a wall.

THE ELASTIC MOMENT

Ice in a glass at the height of a heat wave.
Then a sleep lull that sends you
to the airless inside of a Halloween hat.
Goodnight.

Then a sled, two mittens, and a film
with two women—one black in black satin,
one white wearing pearls—watched
in a paneled room brought in from an era

that's over. Good-bye. Outside,
a dust-covered dog's grave. You, your back
tacked to the seat, basket-weave plastic
on plastic, drive by—your mind

tuned to the news, a glut of miasmic static.
You, a light-bulb filament substitute
for the flame that stands for the awful truth:
the dead of war will now be unknown.

We don't know, the fire says.
At home, the bird's last cuttlebone
is a stripe of white in an empty cage.
Human failings are human failings.

Forgive me.
The streetlamps above emit a halogen haze.
The light makes it easy to think
everything here is reversible.

STUDIES IN NEUROSCIENCE: THE PERPETUAL MOMENT

The mirror is a formula for when the open door
closes on a clock and starts countless wires firing

in rapid succession. The self can't be made visible
outside the brain. Define resuscitative: heart beat

brain bed occupied. Discernable action: the way a,
or the, transparent top of water
in a glass or on a lake sends back light at an angle.

Optics are not always involved
in how others see that face you call your elastic face.

A ROOM IN CLEOPATRA'S PALACE

1.

Flies and a fan and a pillar
in this or that arch of the empire.

Space is such a pain: cars shooting by like bullets,
palm trees pinned against a wall,

a helicopter wasting away the above.
This is the world at one on a street

where the angles of architecture meet
and point west where the end of a tunnel,

unseen but assumed, is draped
with a blanket of crêpe

that it's easy to mistake for night—
[a woman's mouth-made swearing]

CLEOPATRA: And I'm entangled with it.

And now: what to do with the fact
of the once-blue above, the mind cloud

tinted pink with particulate matter—
a pollution that looks like a postcard.

CLEOPATRA: I'm saying yes
to whatever you're saying: an asp in a basket,

betrayal and horror, a room that tilts inward,
natural vice, the smell of sweat, wasted lamps,

petty lives born to murder and war.
The delicate undid disaster of all good things.

2.

The smug see me as nothing but negatives:
    pout-mouth petulance, underwear lust,
a city of mystery in which pathos and greed
    stand empty as high-rent apartments

with coffin-shaped plate glass vents.
    Inside, the dead are resting
on expensive brocade sofas.
    I have stun-gun marks on one arm; there's a fig

at the edge of the myrtle-leaf rug.
    The snake is acting like he likes me.
The dimpled boys are practicing their onion-eyed dirge.
    I don't like it when time ticks back

to where it's just been. It takes stamina to do what I do,
    day after day on my barge.

3.

        During performances, I was devoted
to miming the plans of others: the room,

the walls, the people listening,
the drowning from time to time, whatever.

Watching invariably begins with a glimpse
of awareness, followed by not knowing
what will come after.

I sat in a straight-back chair, lead beneath
my feet. There was a wide arch to the right.

Do you ever think? Yes. No. I don't not
for an instant. I open my eyes,
it's still the present.

                Enter a Messenger

Was this done well?

Who's to say?
Make me up like a manikin
with a cosmetic palette. Tired now?

I know I am. Add a bed, and a sea overtaking
a city. Now draw something
that looks like a blown vent of blood
and a pinching sense of regret
over some wrong done.

COMPULSION IN THEORY AND PRACTICE: PRINCIPLES AND CONTROVERSIES

Psycho-sexual memories coalesce into a complex fear—

I want, I am opposed to—every contrary desire becoming equally evident.

Transference might be a masochistic shame-kiss signifier, or some sort of extreme narcissistic need.

A normal form of defense could lead to a state of rage.

Affective states could be performed on stage.

Chaos could be suggested by something as humble, and as theatrical, as breaking glass.

A human—face painted, dressed as a clock—could race time back to a start line

and then be made to stand, face against the wall, and think and think and think: I am, I never will not be.

HERE'S WHAT THE MAPMAKER KNOWS

O is the ocean and *t* the consequence
of time at the edge of a landscape
of dots plotted into the plane
with a constant scale.

Any place can be located and later divided
by cultural and social data
and sketched on a napkin—
disregarding distance and leaving

only the little one knows.
Description is reductive: a shirt, buttons, a mind
that is willing to enact its own explosive end.
What idiocy the world is made of:

fierce justifications, landmines and such,
a rifle upright. An empire
of uncommon horror: the human speaking,
"Every moment all that matters is me."
Tick-tick in the drifting dark.

SCENE I: A HALL IN THE TEMPLE OF JUSTICE

Verdi refused to write an overture
for *Aïda*, or rather he first wrote a simple prelude
and then replaced it with a potpourri variety
overture but in the end refused to play it
because of its "pretentious insipidity"—
his words, or his words translated into English.
What is translation? What is "insipidity"
in Italian? Aïda is an Ethiopian princess
who is captured and enslaved in Egypt.
It's a story of love and power but then
what story isn't? *O patria mia*. My dear country.

CLOSE OBSERVATION ESPECIALLY OF ONE UNDER SUSPICION

1.

If they want to listen in, I'm happy to allow anyone to overhear a flustered or tormented *I* talking to the other half of my divided self, as if anyone could indict me better. What particulars might capture the excoriating character of the complicated psyche? Someone once said, you—you?—know the body is the site of subjection when the state prints *I see all* as a motto in indelible ink on its money. Is closely observed the same thing as surveillance? If not, in what ways does surveillance differ from simply being watched? Does it matter that the state is doing the watching. Do you care about the ne

2.

The home-made video showed windows. The camera moved too fast to capture people turning on lights or turning off their minds. Some are asleep. It's night now. When I can't turn off my mind and need to sleep, I take a pill until my mind is a pure nothing. The metal cars have all gone. No more reverb. Only a mark where a machine once leaked. Only a deserted walkway leading to a door. The mailbox empty. No mailman in sight. As if the whole world was a lavish myth. When I wake the cars are back in their slots and there's the reek of wa

3.

Where am I, I wondered? A blue light was bouncing against one wall and an edge of the ceiling, which made no sense since the blinds were shut. One of the dresser drawers was pulled out. There was a pile of clothes lying on the floor below it, as if someone had rummaged through the drawer and then fled. I found myself wondering whether there might be ghosts but felt ridiculous for even wondering. And yet, ther

4.

Really, he said, they can listen in. You don't mind? I asked. He said, There has always been an Emperor, only the name changes over time. I thought of the eerie feeling I'd felt in the hotel room, waking that time to find things had been practica

5.

Suddenly you realize, people have been listening to you. You, an open mouth in the middle, plus a shadow that stops the sun and now the shadow is alive inside you. They can see it when you open. Your closed mind won't counteract what is coming up. Counteract: to oppose and obliterate the effect of. No, annihilate. You know what that means. To extinguish. To turn off the light. To turn from one thing into a nothing a

moving through time. Our heads acting
like filters that filter ice in the winter,
cicadas and such in the summer. A system of seeing
through slats. And what is that, that flourish
raising a ruckus of dust? A burr at the sock line
takes a bite. Is that nice? Come here.
Closer. Let's play this way. Like fish that follow
a regular beat. An ear at your chest might make sense
of the beating, but instead, you're face down,
your face facing the fact of the Earth.
Get up. Take a box and fill it with dirt.
Reduce architecture back to a rock and a hard place.
Tuck the idea of a buttress far into the future.
"You can't be there anymore,"
he said. A lobotomy sever between two hemispheres.
The symphony of scalpels quieted.
Peru with one cup of clean water per person.
A sliver of silver in an otherwise empty hand.
Make a landfill that looks like a mountain.
Leaves are falling on only one corner of the intersection.
The cab swings by, takes a turn. And in the back,
dark glasses make moot the issue of eyes. Is this
what you wanted? A boardwalk with wood planks
and squares at the edge, a chrome hat
that comes with a collapsible rabbit.
A hand keeps drawing a card that says go back
to the cell you just flew from. Well, maybe it's not a game
but a coffin cover, the innocence project,
bomb plots and wire strippers. Why make it dirty?
The erotic potential of sheer stupidity,
underneath which is someone in a suicide vest.
The street signs seem both strange and familiar.
In the distance, in a camera flash, dolls dressed in red.

WORN

I'm wearing my waking threadbare
while I'm waking up and walking
in the park. A doctor once told me,
A part of your life will be a room,
a door that's as long as consciousness.
The form of the dream I just had
is a fact. A serious talk. An inner
outward. An animal dead, now
reanimated. Maybe a river, or a lake.
It makes me think that death is a view,
whole, and nothing more tragic
than a species of nonsense where ever
is on a dimmer switch. It's clear
that this lever, this thingness, declines.

THE LAST TWO SECONDS

She was standing as usual, half-sunken in concrete,
uncovered to the summit of August in December,
the broiling furnace of heated winter air blasting past
in front of her like a false wall that holds nothing back.

Impressions approached. Her eyes were level
with the idea behind the scene—a rusted absence
extending back in time. She thought, I will never
step out into this. She felt she was a stick-figure aspect

open to the emporium that sells nothing but combs.
She combed her hair, as if she were safe inside
the iron claw that governs every detail, as if
she had ever been anywhere else. And then like that,

behind a door, she said, someone was drawing
a topographical map where a line turned
into a mountain. In another room, workers were wiring
her body to a machine. The tick was like a metronome,

one tick per second. Nothing was neutral.
Lying on her back, looking up at the glass eye, light
furrowed the future. She saw her own inimitable way
of seeing what is missing and sweeping a floor

and setting up a table and winding a timepiece,
and throwing a voice. When she woke, a rash
was making her a manikin spattered with crimson.
Spatter and drip ripped fabric. An evening collapsed.

A convincing conspiracy of one stood on the blade
of that odd state called over and done with. Outside,
rain at the window created an instant vertical sea.
The land looked like beached long-nose dolphins

stunned into immobility. Lights blinked intermittently
in the haze. She looked back blankly and said, the mind
isn't everything, only a gray-suited troop of mechanics
working to ratchet the self through the teeth of a wheel.

THE DISAPPEARANCE OF AMERIKA: AFTER KAFKA

1. AS SHE "ENTERED NEW YORK HARBOR ON THE NOW SLOW-MOVING SHIP"

A wand was waved. A voice-over said,
"You're going nowhere except where you're led.
Prepare for the future. Prepare for a score."
Composer notes floated in the background.

It was just as much a capital as DC:
declension, dog collar, declawed.
The monument was partially damaged.
A crowd milled at the base.

A press kit promised the trailer would shed light
like a spotlight is known to illuminate a star.
The boat had motored into the harbor,
passing a French woman in green

holding a sword aloft. Was it a sword?
Or a torch? She was no longer sure.
She was here because here is anywhere.
Who hasn't been pushed outside like a cat

that is making a nuisance of itself?
Wasn't she just like everyone else: with a face,
two eyes, one mouth, two air holes, two ears?
Who dares insist on difference?

She overheard someone say, "Well,
that's just how it is, one's own preferences
aren't always taken into account."
To be cast aside "the way one throws out a cat

when it becomes annoying."
To be divinely young.
That was the essence of a "summer house,"
wasn't it?—a window opened out onto a meadow,

which led to a river (linear and male), or a lake
(circular and female), whatever you wished.
Her eagerness was earnest
and fit with fashionable attitudes.

The knowledge of failure
was in the distance, or at the bottom
of a glass—a beverage that left a trace
at her lip line. A hand wiped the trace away.

Her best hope was that on the first floor
there would be someone who might serve
as a model. Yet, she thought,
one mustn't be naïve about motives,

since they are always mixed.
There were so many things to consider:
the feel of a faux-leather sofa, the picture
of a perfect apple, shrink-wrapped in plastic.

Who didn't consider oneself a guerilla band,
heroically battling regular forces.
The needs of the moment were ever-pressing,
yes, but so was her love of the underdog.

Which would she choose?
And who's to say she had a choice?
Chance only sometimes branched
in front of her like a limited fish fork.

This way was X, that way was Y.
She might lie down and sleep
on a pile of clothes taken from the closet.
Or on a loveseat still warm from a woman

who had acted as if she were queen.
In the past, each time she woke, she was
in trouble again. In spite of best efforts,
she often made the wrong friends.

The dragnet closed in around her.
Once caught, she'd never escape.
The key wasn't where it should be.
"Should be?" Or was it "could be"?

Another small error to add to the others.
She knew there was no ending
to the ever-ongoing. She had begun
with hope and a house. Some minor act

was misread and—*alley-oop*—
that knocked the lead domino down.
She knew little more than when she had started.
That said, it wasn't that she knew nothing,

it was just that what must be known
was constantly evolving. Yes, that was it.
She sat on the love seat. She ate a chocolate
arranged around a walnut. She wondered
when they invented such emptiness.

2. SHE FOUND HERSELF "BEING PUSHED GRADUALLY TOWARD THE RAIL BY AN EVER-SWELLING THRONG"

What she was certain of was this:
the awful unknown would continue
to complicate the facts and meanwhile,
one had to distract oneself. In the meanwhile,

or for a few more weeks, she said,
I'll simply act as if I belong here. How unkind
to have a brain that could only recall
that day dissolved into evening, or

that the neighbor on the balcony knew nothing
but pain and prodding. Of course,
there was the panic of the lost bag.
It was finally found, yes—what luck!—

but the story of worry continued to exist:
daylight out the window faded
while the human element was speaking.
There was also the very pushy uncle

who had promised to be a savior but then,
on a whim, retracted the promise.
She said, "We drank ginger lemonade,
then watched a movie with a plot

that was messy but inspiring."
What more could one want
except for time to go by in thirty-minute intervals.
Each wasn't enough—but still

the undercurrent was the terror one lived with
while doing what she couldn't remember.
She was always there and always
answering questions and entertaining

at a party that relieved her
from the plight of being herself.
You could call it a ballet: cooking, clean up,
cooking, repeat. On and on. A broken glass

on the edge of boredom, on the way
to becoming. Why was that disconcerting?
Because she knew that between effort and effect,
there was mystery. And inevitably,

some bad luck. Going backward was pure panic,
a 3 a.m. moment wrapped in an anxious blanket.
It consoled not at all that next door,
in the taller of two apartment buildings, there

was someone who looked like the self she had been
before time had made several revisions.
More and more time passed.
In the mirror, where her face should have been,

was the small clay box she had made in first grade—
its terrible childish beauty, its hopeful moment.
She set it on a table, as painful as that was.
The ballet was bleak, the bed in the corner

was a symbol of what she didn't know.
She told herself she was lucky she had so little support
because it meant she had little to lose.
Someone suggested she try to be less guarded,

simply make the elevator go up and down.
And yet, didn't up and down exist in the same space—
so where had she been, really?
Outside, a snow and ice storm. Or was it inside?

A massive blood rush above a face
that was papered onto an oval head
that was slightly atilt, as if the mouth was about
to push out a question. Sadly, the question

had already been answered and not in her favor.
On Tuesday she considered going back to last week
and starting over. Perhaps in Chicago,
where winters were cold as Lake Cocytus.

Perhaps in Tulsa, in an empty mansion
built by an absent oil baron. Perhaps
she would bounce from one city to the next
for all of March and half of April,

staying in bare-bone motels
near shuttered airports. It all blurred.
Why not stay where she was
and spend time with strangers?

Of course some were slightly tense and a few
were bitter. She needed to remember,
she was as much a cipher to them
as they were to her. Who wasn't living

on the opposite side of non-existence?
Cultivating one's past damage while watching
the doorman at the hotel next door
hail a cab for a woman
who was holding a poodle. Arf. Arf, arf.

3. THE MISSING PERSON

Today had dissolved into nothing worthwhile:
small tasks, a vague sense of indignation
at having been ignored on the street
by a child at whom she had smiled.

At least she thought she had smiled.
She partnered with the harpies in her head.
They showed her short films of every error
she'd ever made. Remember this,

they asked? And this? They never tired.
They showed her Darwin's last daydream.
It was a tour of his childhood:
a miniature lake, a park named January,

a frozen road, the corner of a hill.
The Monday loaf of bread seemed enormous
now, like a dead armadillo.
She said, "A border is forever moving away,

and as it moves, the individual begins to bleed
into the landscape."
She said, "I don't even know what I'm saying
except a single life seems like a false construct.

Each individual is so interconnected
there is barely anything that can properly be
called a self." The backdrop was a drape
on which was written grim statistics

about wars she'd experienced vicariously,
making each singular death both real
and a figment of her over-anxious imagination,
which doubled the tragedy of the irrevocable

outcome. She sat at the edge of a circle.
The engineer wore a doctor's white coat
and told her that she might be in the midst
of a migraine and to simply drag herself

from place to place via subway, bus, or by taxi.
This was the punishment she deserved.
The dour waitress wasn't the problem.
There were periodic questions: is this true,

has this documentary—in which
the scaffolding crashes—been tampered with?
Did this melodrama happen?
Or was it fiction installed like a furnace

to warm the house?
Bewilderment could fuse everything together.
How was she sleeping? She said her dreams
seemed quaint and mannered,

and had nothing to say about the world of now.
Yes, cowardly political forces stood in the way
of right, but was that something new?
The cruelty. The hubris. The insane selfishness.

Incarceration as a form of colonization.
Blatant racism and sexism
that went unpunished, and thus prompted more.
To give up, she knew, would be to say uncle

to the aching. In makeup,
someone smeared color on her face
leaving her feeling even more self-conscious.
Life was testing her indulgence.

If only she could enjoy being an animal,
kept busy with being alive. But instead,
the body politic was a perpetual pain machine.
You could lie down on it, or under it.

It was an architectural wonder, an indie film
called *The Disappearance*. In a pit,
the pendulum scratched the tender surface.
Was it a question of daring to cross

some dangerous line? Of allowing a thought train
to take up the fragments of a difficult life
and imagine what constant anxiety felt like.
To live in that state, crying for the lack of comfort.

The continual dread. The belated beginning.
The damaged family. The early ruin.
The history of work under a brutal sun.
In a steel trap of tiny tomorrows, she sat
in the shade and waited to escape this mind set.

FILMING THE DOOMSDAY CLOCK

We were told that the cloud cover was a blanket
about to settle into the shape of the present
which, if we wanted to imagine it
as a person, would undoubtedly look startled—
as after a verbal berating
or in advance of a light pistol-whipping.
The camera came and went, came and went,
like a masked man trying to light a too-damp fuse.
The crew was acting like a litter of mimics
trying to make a killing.
Anything to fill the vacuum of time.
The wind whirred and tracked the clouds.
The credits, we were told, would take the form
of a semi-scrawl, urban-sprawl, graffiti-style
typography. The soundtrack would include
instrumental versions of "Try a Little Tenderness."
Our handler, who was walking backward
in order to maintain constant eye contact with us,
nearly stumbled over a girl in a sheath and pearls
who was misting a shelf of hothouse flowers.
While the two apologized to each other,
we stood and watched the fine spray settle
over the leaves and drip onto the floor.
On the way out, we passed a door
with a small window reinforced with wired glass
through which we could see a nurse
positioning a patient on a table. We swore
afterward we'd heard her say, "Lie perfectly still
and look only inward." A clock chimed and
as the others were audibly counting backwards
from five to zero, I thought I heard someone say,
"Now let go of this morbid attachment to things."

NOTES

The cover image, *Speeding Monorail: On the Precipice* by Kikuzo Ito, illustrated a magazine article, "World Transportation Invention Competition," in a 1936 issue of *Shonen Club*, a Japanese boys' magazine.

The Earthquake She Slept Through: *The Metamorphosis* by Franz Kafka tells the story of Gregor Samsa, a traveling salesman who wakes to find he has turned into a giant insect. When he fails to leave for work on time, his sister Greta talks to him through his closed bedroom, asking, "*Ist dir nicht wohl? Brauchst du etwas?*" (Are you not well? Is there anything you want?)

Costumes Exchanging Glances: Bertrand Russell said, "Electricity is not a thing like St. Paul's Cathedral; it is a way in which things behave." Walter Benjamin said, "Things are only mannequins and even the great world-historical events are only costumes beneath which they exchange glances with nothingness, with the base and the banal." Walter Benjamin, *Protocols to the Experiments on Hashish, Opium and Mescaline 1927–1934*, "Protocol II: Highlights of the Second Hashish Impression," 1928, trans. Scott J. Thompson, 1997.

You Know: The poem is an ekphrastic response to Jessica Stockholder's outdoor sculpture *Flooded Chambers Maid*, mixed media installation, 2009–2010. This poem, along with "In This Box," "The Elastic Moment," "A Technical Drawing of the Moment," "An Autopsy of an Era," "Scene I: A Hall in the Temple of Justice," "The Numbers," and "A Structure of Repeating Units," first appeared in *Jessica Stockholder: Grab Grassy This Moment Your I's: Assemblages by Jessica Stockholder*, poems by Mary Jo Bang. St. Louis Laumeier Sculpture Park, 2011, published in conjunction with the exhibition, *Jessica Stockholder: Grab Grassy This Moment Your I's*, February 12 to May 29, 2011.

Masquerade: After Beckmann: Max Beckmann, *Masquerade*, oil on canvas, 1948.

The Storm We Call Progress: The title is taken from Walter Benjamin's 1940 essay, "On the Concept of History," in which he describes a painting by Paul Klee: "There is a painting by Klee called *Angelus Novus*. It shows an angel who seems about to move away from something he stares at. His eyes are wide, his mouth is open, his wings are spread. This is how the angel of history must look. His face is turned toward the past. Where a chain of events appears before *us, he* sees one single catastrophe, which keeps piling wreckage upon wreckage and hurls it at his feet. The angel would like to stay, awaken the dead, and make whole what has been smashed. But a storm is blowing from Paradise and has got caught in his wings; it is so strong that the angel can no longer close them. This storm drives him irresistibly into the future to which his back is turned, while the pile of debris before him grows toward the sky. What we call progress is *this* storm." Walter Benjamin, *Selected Writings*, Vol. 4: 1938–1940, trans. Harry Zohn (Cambridge: Harvard University Press, 2003).

Some of the language, including this list—"varicose veins, rubber knickers, douches with bulbs, douches with bags, girdles in a choice of pink, red or white, and in rubber, silk or twilled linen, enemas, clysters . . . etc."—comes from a translation by Simon-Watson Taylor (*Paris Peasant*, Picador: 1980) of Louis Aragon's Surrealist text *Le Paysan de Paris* (Gallimard: 1926). Walter Benjamin's *Das Passagen-Werk* (*The Arcades Project*) was influenced by Aragon's book. "Benjamin etceteras" echoes the end of Aragon's list, and includes the many items that fill Benjamin's *The Arcades Project*.

Sturm und Drang (*Storm and Stress*) is a term that refers both to the title of a 1776 play by Friedrich von Klinger and to a German literary movement that flourished in the 1770's. The literature and music responded to Enlightenment ideals of a humane society that elevated the social and moral good (reason and tolerance) over prejudice and religious ideology. It was also a protest against the oppressive restrictions of tradition in a system defined by a powerful aristocracy and a vast peasant underclass.

"He stared sadly at the ruins of his house" is a usage example taken from the German translation for the word *sad* from *Cambridge Dictionaries Online*: http://dictionary.cambridge.org/us/dictionary/english-german/sad.

Provisional Doubt as an Architectural Space: The poem takes language from Raphael Rubinstein's article "Provisional Painting Part 2: To Rest Lightly on Earth" in *Art in America*, February 1, 2012. The poem is dedicated to him.

Lions and Tigers: The Escaped Animal Was Bent to the Trainer's Will: The poem's title is a photo caption on page 83 of a "Little Big Book" titled

Lions and Tigers: With Clyde Beatty (With pictures from the Carl Loemmie production "The Big Cage." Based on the story "The Big Cage" by Edward Anthony) (Whitman Publishing: Racine, Wisconsin, 1934). Thanks to Carl Phillips for the book.

The poem was originally posted at 350.org on October 24, 2009, as part of an "International Day of Climate Action."

The Blank of Reason Produces Blank: After Goya: The poem title alters the English title of an etching by Francisco de Goya y Lucientes: *The Sleep of Reason Produces Monsters (El sueño de la razon produce monstruos)*, Plate 43 of *Los Caprichos (The Caprices)*, etching, aquatint, drypoint, and burin, 1799.

The *chorda tympani* is a branch of the facial nerve that travels through the middle ear and crosses the tympanic membrane (eardrum).

In Dante's *Inferno*, Canto XIII, line 84, Dante says to Virgil, *"ch'i' non potrei, tanta pietà m'accora"* (For I cannot, such pity is in my heart.)—trans. Henry Wadsworth Longfellow.

Let's Say Yes: The six poems in this series were composed of words found in a 296-page paperback edition of *Mrs. Dalloway* by Virginia Woolf (A Harvest/HBJ Book, Harcourt Brace Javanovich, New York and London: 1985). "Scene after Scene" uses words found on pages 1–50; "This Bell Like a Bee Striking," pages 50–100; "The Nerve Fibers," pages 100–150; "To Write a History," pages 150–200; "Opened and Shut," pages 200–250; and "There She Was," pages 250–296.

Explain the Brain: The title of the poem and some of its language is taken from Carl F. Craver's *Explaining the Brain: Mechanisms and the Mosaic Unity of Neuroscience* (Oxford University Press, 2009). The book is concerned with neuroscientific explanations of causality, especially how to determine which ideas are logically sound and which are not. He invokes Aristotle's example of something that is associated with the sunrise but doesn't "explain" it (a rooster's almost invariable crowing at dawn) and compares that to Sylvain Bromberger's example of something that does in fact mirror the explanation of the sunrise—changes in the length of a shadow cast by a flagpole as the sun moves higher in the sky.

All through the Night: The title, and *We have no past we won't reach back,* is taken from the song "All through the Night" on Cyndi Lauper's 1983 debut album, *She's So Unusual.* (Words and original music by Jules Shear.)

Pussy Riot, a social-activist feminist punk rock group, partly inspired by the 1990's Riot Grrrl movement in the US, was founded in Moscow in 2011. On February 21, 2012, to protest the re-election of Vladimir Putin, the group entered a near-empty Russian Orthodox Cathedral in Moscow and danced up to the altar while singing a brief expletive-laced song with the refrain "Holy Mother, send Putin packing!" Three of the group's members, Maria Alyokhina, Nadezhda Tolokonnikova, and Yekaterina Samutsevich, were later arrested and charged with "premeditated hooliganism." All three were found guilty and sentenced to two years in a penal colony. In October 2012, Yekaterina Samutsevich was released on appeal; in December, 2014, in advance of the 2014 Sochi Winter Olympics, the remaining two women were released in a general amnesty for non-violent offenders and mothers of young children.

Reading Conrad's *Heart of Darkness*: In spite of a multilateral CITES (Convention on International Trade in Endangered Species of Wild Fauna and Flora) treaty that went into effect in 1975, continued demand for elephant-ivory products has resulted in a global underground economy that fuels poaching in Africa and Asia and threatens large numbers of elephants.

As in Corona: The poem takes some of its language from entries in *Volume VI: Comines to Deaf-Mute* of the *Funk & Wagnall's Universal Standard Encyclopedia* (c. 1953–56). It was originally commissioned by Mel Chin and Nick Flynn for Mel Chin's encyclopedia collage project (published as *The Funk & Wag from A to Z,* Menil Collection: 2014). Thanks to both of them.

A Room in Cleopatra's Palace: Shakespeare's *Antony and Cleopatra* begins: "Scene I. Alexandria. A room in Cleopatra's palace."

Scene I: A Hall in the Temple of Justice: *Aïda,* a four-act opera with music composed by Giuseppe Verdi, libretto by Antonio Ghislanzoni (after a scenario by Auguste Mariette), begins: "Scene I: A hall in the Temple of Justice." The opera was first performed at the Cairo Opera House on December 24, 1871. A 1953 film version of the opera starred Sophia Loren as Aïda, an Ethiopian slave; the music was lip-synched. *O patria mia* (Oh, my country) is part of an aria that Aïda, who is in love with her Egyptian captor, sings in the third act.

Close Observation Especially of One under Suspicion: The title is taken from the definition of *surveillance—Noun*: close observation or supervision maintained over a person, group, etc, esp one in custody or under suspicion—found in Dictionary.com. *Collins English Dictionary: Complete & Unabridged*, 10th Edition. HarperCollins Publishers. http://dictionary.reference.com/browse/surveillance (accessed: July 10, 2014).

Sure, it's a little game. You, me, our minds: The poem was written as the first part of a six-part exquisite corpse published in *Tin House* for an issue called "Games People Play" (No. 43, 2010). The other participants were Nick Flynn, Matthea Harvey, Alex Lemon, Eileen Myles, and D. A. Powell. Thanks to Poetry Editor Brenda Shaughnessy.

The Innocence Project, founded in 1992 by Barry C. Scheck and Peter J. Neufeld at the Benjamin N. Cardozo School of Law at Yeshiva University, helps prisoners prove their innocence through DNA testing. The Project has helped to exonerate more than three hundred people in the US, including eighteen who had served time on death row. The average time between imprisonment and exoneration and release has been thirteen years.

An Individual Equinox Suitable for Framing: The poem is for Kathleen Finneran.

The Disappearance of Amerika: After Kafka: The quoted material in the subtitles is taken from Mark Harman's 2008 translation of Franz Kafka's unfinished novel *Amerika*. Written between 1911 and 1914, Kafka had intended the book to be titled *Der Verschollene* (*The Missing Person* or *The Man Who Disappeared*); his literary executor Max Brod changed it to *Amerika*. The first chapter was published in Germany in 1913 as *Der Heizer* (*The Stoker*).

Filming the Doomsday Clock: The Doomsday Clock is a clock face that was established in 1947 by an international group of scientists called Chicago Atomic Scientists. It has appeared since then on every cover of the *Bulletin of the Atomic Scientists*. The hands are set closer or farther from midnight depending upon political—and since 2007, ecological—global events that threaten the planet. On January 14, 2014, it was set at five minutes to midnight.

An earlier version of this poem was published as "Doktor Strangelove." The 1964 Stanley Kubrick film *Dr. Strangelove, or How I Learned to Stop Worrying and Love the Bomb* starred Peter Sellers. An instrumental version of "Try a Little Tenderness" played during the opening credits. Kubrick, describing the development of the script said, "And it was at this point I decided to treat the story as a nightmare comedy. Following this approach, I found it never interfered with presenting well-reasoned arguments. In culling the incongruous, it seemed to me to be less stylized and more realistic than any so-called serious, realistic treatment, which in fact is more stylized than life itself by its careful exclusion of the banal, the absurd, and the incongruous. In the context of impending world destruction, hypocrisy, misunderstanding, lechery, paranoia, ambition, euphemism, patriotism, heroism, and even reasonableness can evoke a grisly laugh."

ACKNOWLEDGMENTS

Thanks to the editors of the following journals where these poems appeared, sometimes in an earlier version:

Asymptote (online): "Close Observation Especially of One under Suspicion"; *The Awl* (online): "An Autopsy of an Era," "The Numbers," and "The Storm We Call Progress"; *The Believer*: "Wall Street"; *Better Magazine* (online): "A Structure of Repeating Units" and "A Technical Drawing of the Moment"; *Boston Review*: "The Nerve Fibers"; *Brand Literary Magazine* (UK): "Silence Always Happens Suddenly"; *Conduit*: "Here's What the Mapmaker Knows"; *Crazyhorse*: "Scene I: A Hall in the Temple of Justice," "In This Box" and "Studies in Neuroscience: The Perpetual Moment"; *Critical Quarterly* (UK): "The Disappearance of Amerika: After Kafka"; *Denver Quarterly*: "The Too-Bright Light Will Wash You Out," "The Perpetual Night She Went Into," "The Landscapist," "Except for Being, It Was Relatively Painless," and "As in Corona"; *Fence*: "Two Places and One Time," "Two Frames," and "Under the Influence of Ideals"; *Harvard Review*: "Silence Always Happens Suddenly"; *Hazlitt* (Random House in Canada): "A Man Mentioned in an Essay"; *Health & Spirituality*: "Explain the Brain"; *Island* (Australia): "The Storm We Call Progress"; *jubilat*: "Scene after Scene," "Opened and Shut," "Equidistant from the Center of Never," "The earthquake in this case was," and "Had There Been"; *The Kenyon Review*: "A Calculation Based on Figures in a Scene," "To Write a History," "There She Was," and "Can the Individual Experience Tragic Consequences?"; *Lo-Ball* Magazine: "Masquerade: After Beckmann"; *The New Republic*: "Rude Mechanicals" and "An Individual Equinox Suitable for Framing"; *The New Yorker*: "The Circus Watcher" and "All through the Night"; *Ploughshares*: "At the Moment of Beginning" and "Practice for Being Empty"; *Poetry London* (UK): "The Elastic Moment," "The Last Two Seconds," "Time Trap: The Perpetual Moment," and "Worn"; *Salmagundi*: "Provisional Doubt as an Architectural Space" and "Reading Conrad's *Heart of Darkness*"; *Thumbnail Magazine*: "Lions and Tigers: The Escaped Animal Was Bent to the Trainer's Will"; *Tin House*: "Sure, it's a little game. You, me, our minds"; *Vanitas*: "Compulsion in Theory and Practice: Principles and Controversies," "Studies in Neuroscience: The Perpetual Moment," and "Filming the Doomsday Clock" (published as "Doktor Strangelove"); *WQS: Women's Cultural Studies*: "This Bell Like a Bee Striking"; *The Yale Review*: "A Room in Cleopatra's Palace."

"The Earthquake She Slept Through," "You Know," and "Costumes Exchanging Glances" appeared on *Poem-A-Day*, an online publication of the Academy of American Poets. "Under the Influence of Ideals" was reprinted in *American Poet* Fall/Winter 2013.

Many thanks to Aníbal Cristobo, publisher and translator, and Patricio Grinberg, translator, of *El Claroscuro del Pinguino: Antología Poética Bilingüe* (kriller71ediciones, 2013), and to Luna Miguel, for the introduction. Some of these poems were included in that book. Thanks to Mariagiorgia Ulbar for translating some of these poems into Italian, and to Annette Kühn for translating some into German.

Thanks also to Hand Held Editions (and Poetry Editors Tom Hummel and Brett Fletcher Lauer) for printing the six poems in the series titled *Let's Say Yes* as a chapbook.

Thanks to Andrew Ridker for including "The Storm We Call Progress" in *Privacy Policy: The Anthology of Surveillance Poetics* (Black Ocean, 2014).

Forever-thanks to family and to friends, especially to Mark Bibbins, Timothy Donnelly, Kathleen Finneran, Jennifer Kronovet, Lynn Melnick, Marjorie Perloff, David Schuman, and Mónica de la Torre. More thanks to Bill Clegg, and to Jeff Shotts and everyone at Graywolf Press who helped these poems become a book. Thanks also to Yuki Tanaka for locating Daisuke Ito, and to Daisuke Ito for permission to use the cover image.

Mary Jo Bang is the author of six previous poetry collections, including *Elegy*, winner of the National Book Critics Circle Award and a *New York Times* Notable Book. She has also published an acclaimed new translation of Dante's *Inferno*. Bang has received a fellowship from the Guggenheim Foundation, a Hodder Fellowship from Princeton University, and a Berlin Prize Fellowship from the American Academy in Berlin. She is a professor of English and teaches in the creative writing program at Washington University in Saint Louis.

Book design by Connie Kuhnz. Composition by Bookmobile Design and Digital Publisher Services, Minneapolis, Minnesota. Manufactured by Versa Press on acid-free, 30 percent postconsumer wastepaper.